VIGNETTES FROM THE FRONT

The World War I Diary
of Lieutenant Colonel Joseph Twyman

Anne Price

Book design by Richard Fenwick at Good Looking Books

ISBN: 978-1-5431-5274-6

It is my honor to dedicate this book
to Dorsey Price, my husband,
who encouraged me to tell this story.

Captain Dorsey D. Price graduated from the Air Force Academy in 1966. As an Air Force fighter pilot, Dorsey flew over 2,000 hours in the F-4 Phantom, and was awarded the Distinguished Flying Cross during the Vietnam War. He served with great distinction with all the others who fought for our country during that war.

Captain Joseph Twyman in France, 1917

VIGNETTES FROM THE FRONT

The World War I Diary
of Lieutenant Colonel Joseph Twyman

ONE

"Over There" may be just a song that you may have heard over the years about the call to arms sending our country's men to the Western Front to fight the Germans.

The story that I am about to tell is almost 100 years old, but our future generations need to know what it was like for many of us Doughboys in what is known as The Great War from 1914 to 1918.

I was just a soldier from Horsecave, Kentucky, who ran away from Normal (teachers) school at the age of 17 in 1900 to join the army and was accepted. The training was harder than I had expected, so I confessed that I had lied when I had enlisted. The Commander wrote to my father in Kentucky, who wrote back that whatever age I had given, that was my age. So I was stuck. That decision by my father changed the direction of my life.

On June 8, 1917, I was appointed Second Lieutenant Cavalry assigned to Fort Williams, Maine, to be prepared for overseas duty. After bidding my dear wife and babies farewell it was time to go to Fort Adams, Rhode Island, and then on to New York City. On August 18th we were transferred to the Cunard Steamer, Aurania.

Standing on the deck of the Aurania troop ship with my fellow soldier Nick, I said: "What the hell did we get ourselves into?" We were in a convoy of other ships to battle the Germans on the Western Front.

Thinking back to kissing my wife Flora and the babies goodbye at the train station, I pictured her handing me her rosary, kissing it saying "Holy Mary, Mother of God please protect my Joe." I held back my tears in order to look strong to my little family as the train pulled out of the station. I can still hear the band playing the wartime favorite, "Over there, the Yanks are coming." Now I was a Yank instead of a Southerner. Looking up at the stars my fear was that I would not be a brave enough soldier to protect my men, make the world safe for Democracy and still return home to my family.

The wind was blowing off the open deck reminding me of the nights when I was a boy on the farm back in Kentucky. Every night while on the deck I desperately wanted a cigarette. However, smoking was not allowed at night on the open deck so that the ship would be as invisible as possible to the German submarines. The punishment for such an act was severe. I would take swigs of whiskey from my flask and head down to my bunk, which was 6 feet long, my exact height. My pillow was a life preserver that I hoped I would not have to use.

Nick grumbled loudly when he tried out his bunk for the first time. He was 6'2" and weighted 200 pounds. Luckily, he was on the bottom bunk. He was from Up-State New York where his family grew grapes. We would laugh at each other's accents. This was the first time either one of us had been out to sea, as it was for the other thousands of men on these troop ships. We would experience rough water, seasickness and the constant fear of attack from the Germans.

Sometimes at night before kneeling down for nightly prayers I would try to find a little light under the covers to read the Little Willy silly poem like this one: "

<blockquote>
Willy had the baby's ear
Firmly to the chandelier
Baby chuckled, full of flee:
'twas his ear of corn, you see"
</blockquote>

(Poem published in the *Los Angeles Herald*, 1906)

In my pocket was a booklet that was given to us as we were about to cross the Atlantic. We were warned that the journey would not be an easy one. There would be crossed conditions, and if attacked by German U-boats we could even die at sea. The time on the sea gave me time to reflect upon what fate could be awaiting us when the crossing was complete. For all of us it was a daily struggle to keep our heads up. We were told that the voyage could last from 10 days to three weeks. I had been an active soldier and to stay in such close quarters, unable to take action, would test my inner strength. I remember playing football back in 1907 with the Army team at Fort Revere, Massachusetts. My fellow teammates did not know the battle that we would be facing in only 10 years. We were all so full of piss and vinegar.

We arrived at Halifax, Nova Scotia, having nice weather and lifeboat drills daily. We joined a convoy of 7 ships and left the following day. There were 2000 soldier aboard our ship. I am in command of a large boat that held 64 people. It was so cold we wore overcoats. The sea was rough with lots of seasickness. August 29th four British destroyers met us for guards, and we were glad to see them. On August 30th a German sub came very close but did not attack.

Late in the day we docked in Bantry Bay, County Cork, Ireland, because the Germans knew we were one of the ships on the way to the Front. As we then continued on, a steamer passed us that just an hour later would be attacked by a sub and all would be killed. Seeing the remains of the ship and the floating bodies as we passed, we were reminded of what we were facing even before being on the battlefield. I looked up to the sky and said a quick prayer asking for His protection for all on board.

The next day a torpedo was fired at us and missed us by only about 600 yards. We slept on deck with our clothes on each night. With the wind blowing swiftly, my hat blew off. One of my fellow soldiers sold me one of his. He said to me, "Hey Joe, why do you need another hat?" Then he looked up at my bald head and joked, "Oh, I see, to keep your head warm."

While shivering on deck I thought I joined the Army to fight on the ground, not to be in the Navy surrounded by water with no way to escape. This was a tough war that was fought on the ground, sea and air. The United States had a lot of catching up to do in that we were not prepared for such a war across the sea.

Our next stop was in Liverpool, England, where we were sent to Camp Borden, Hampshire, South Southwest London. Due to rationing there was very little food. As I looked at the tin plate in front of me with just a little porridge, salt port and dry bread, I missed my momma's cracklin' cornbread, beans, greens and buttermilk that I did not appreciate at the time. Sadly, this was not time for thoughts of the old farm life.

When we were settled, Captain Parton, HMS, took me to dinner to a cafe with roast beef, potatoes and some real Scotch Whiskey. There would be many times on the battlefield that my mouth would water at recalling that meal. I can still hear the Captain's voice saying "Hey Mate, what is it like in a big city like New York? Are the women as beautiful as I have heard?" As we drove in his jeep I enjoyed for a short time being on the Famous Hogs Back Road. When it was time to break camp, the journey to the Front would take us to Havre, France.

Along the road we would see German prisoners who thought that we were the British. We were wondering what would it be like to be captured by the Germans? Would it be better to be killed quickly or to be starved and tortured by the enemy? That question was on all of our minds.

TWO

From being on a large ship now our method of travel would be a dinky little train that would take us to Mially, Aube France, where we would establish our Brigade Headquarters. This would be where we would prepare to further advance into enemy territory. Troops from around the world were housed and readied for combat.

In that we were the first Americans, the French more than welcomed us. They would do without so that we would have plenty. The trip over and across was over now with our convoys of protective ships heading off the German subs. I prayed that God would protect us and be merciful to all.

My position was as Brigade Transportation officer, to include electric lighting and telephone equipment. We would have 38 autos, 20 trucks, and 45 motorcycles with sidecars. This was not my training in the Regular Army, but when given duty, it is an order to be followed.

Now that I was in France I felt the need to be at mass and communion each Sunday when possible. Being in the old churches gave me a feeling of peace, if only for an hour. Of course I could not understand the priest in that I did not speak French but the Latin was familiar to me.

One of my prayers was answered when I was relieved from being the transportation officer and placed in command of my old Battery G 7th Artillery. This was an honor being with many of my men when we were given guns and would drill on them daily. Nick, my ship friend, greeted me saying, "Hey Joe I thought we were going to play a little football for recreation till I found out they meant soccer, Ugh."

Fighting the war would cost American money that it did not have. The Federal Income Tax would cover part of the cost, but the remainder of the price tag would be met by the selling of war bonds that would be called Liberty-loans. Movie stars back in the states like Douglas Fairbanks and Mary Pickford donated their time and talent to rallies aimed at selling bonds as quickly as possible. As to our unit, every officer and man in our regiment took at least one bond to qualify 100% subscription. General John Pershing mentioned our regiment in orders from the General Headquarters for this achievement.

The Battery Moved to Houssimont, Marne, near the old Somme Battlefield. On Christmas day I broke down and cried in my hut after coming back from mass. The ordeal was terrible. God only knew how I longed for Flora and my babies. My best attempt would be a feeble expression of what I had in my heart molded by my wife's loving hands.

As a Catholic, at times I questioned God's part in this war when I knelt down to pray at night. Then I remembered before getting on the ship my priest said to me, "Joe, in John 15 from the Bible, 'Greater love hat no man than this, that a man lay down his life for his friends.'" I look at my country as my friends.

On the 1st of January, the Colonel sent us up on a plane for the first time. He took me aside and looked me in my eyes as he said, "Our young men came to war to escape the daily boredom of their clerking, I hope they are ready for what is ahead." As Nick and I looked down over the wings he exclaimed, "Do you think it is safer to be up in the sky where Germans could miss us, or in the trenches to be shot and buried?"

After days getting practice with our firearms we got to go to the beautiful city of Reims that was almost in ruins. However, the Cathedral where all of the Kings of France were crowned was still standing. I picked up a piece of German shell where Joan of Arc stood when Charles VII was crowned King.

The battles were heating up, so I was sent to Army heavy artillery school at Mially. I received $253 for commanding the battery of which I bought a diamond ring for Flora for 750 francs. Each Sunday I went to communion thinking of my wife and two children who were now receiving their first holy communion. There was plenty of love and blessings bestowed upon me this day and I was ashamed of my tears before those who do not understand , but proud and glad in my heart that they came freely.

After all of our practice drills with the French we were all ready to go into action against the Germans. We blew up a portion of their trenches in just 12 minutes. It was then time for us to construct dugouts 15 feet underground in case the Germans returned fire. This was hard work for the men who were eager to begin firing.

Later one night we heard a thunderstorm crash in our ears. A young private began to cry "Mom, Man." He had not been hit but was fearful with a wail that seemed older than the world.

The highlight of the day would be when we received letters from home. I would tear open an envelope to read from my own Flora's hand as to what her life was like back in Portland, Maine with our three small children.

Here is one letter held to my chest after digesting every word:

My dear Doc (her nickname for me),

> *Every day I hear fellow Americans clamoring for victory. The slogans for the day are: Win the war. Beat back the Hun. Save food. Buy bonds. Give till it hurts."*
>
> *I go to mass to pray for you. The children and I go to the moving pictures just to forget that you are fighting for our country and our Allies against the Germans. At the theatre we were asked to enroll in the Food Administration by signing a Food Pledge Card, eating less meat, sugar, wheat and pork so that you men will be properly fed. We were asked to sign the pledge card at the door upon leaving, and mail it before going to bed that night.*
>
> *We have zero weather. The nights are so cold all four of us cuddle up on one bed. Oh, how I miss your warm strong body next to me. It is so cold that today I was glad to be able to buy 1700 pounds of coal for our cook stove. At times there are orders restricting the use of coal so it is good to have it in advance.*
>
> *Doc, I know that we Americans at home are not sleeping in mud, not lying in caverns with thunder and lightening above. We are not munching on a cracker and a piece of cold bacon nor standing gun in hand with the fear of death around the hill. We are not giving our all for America, but are doing the best we can.*
>
> *May God be with you and bring you home safely.*

I love you,
Your Flora.

January, 1918

The letter that I would write back to Flora could not tell her of the details of our life on the Front. The censors read all correspondence that we would send, which I understand.

THREE

Many days were uneventful, filled with trivial events, repetitive training and mindless labor. All at once we would be ordered to move from place to place with reasons that were not clear. Even in the water soaked trenches our men would spend days or weeks with nothing happening but being cold, hungry, wearing filthy tattered clothes and covered at night with mud caked blankets.

At the edge of the fighting zone I looked up to see aircraft diving and turning into dog fights, hoping that when a flaming plane went down it was one of theirs not ours. One night we were awakened by a thump just outside of our sleeping area. Then we saw a pilot crawling out from under the scorched torn parachute. In his pain he cried out, "Lieutenant, I am alive! The average expectancy of a pilot on the Western Front is three weeks. I beat it. I am lucky to be alive to fight another day."

Just as we were trying to get a little shuteye I noticed Private Mason putting a razor edge on his bayonet ready for the morning attack. He growled, "They can't come too thick or too fast. They've been sneering at what we Yankees were going to do in this war, and it's about time they get punctures in their tires."

From a distance, a flash in the sky rose over a barren stretch of no-mans land that separated the hostile forces. I yelled out to my men: "The Germans are right on the job with their fireworks, men fix your bayonets."

Another order was given, "Put on your gas masks." The men looked like a long line of goblins.

The battle was about to begin.

The first barrage from my Battery opened fire on a four gun German battery with 200 high explosive shells. Some distance off we could hear the sounds of voices in guttural tones, the occasional click of a bayonet as it was slipped into place and the low rumble of what might have been field pieces being moved into place.

My men were in a nerve-trying situation, but life or death would depend on their self-control. Private Mason almost broke a blood vessel as he was trying to hold back a strong desire to sneeze. I gave the order, "Have your guns ready men, be prepared to fire the last shell. Then the Germans opened up with several batteries of shrapnel on us. We all had beat it into our dugouts and did not get caught but crazy Shaunnasy ran out and shouted, "You bastard Heinies, take this," and fired our last shell back to them. The Germans did not do any great damage but ruined my portable kitchen pots and pans, which ruined our supper.

As harrowing as the day had been, our men were too young and healthy to stand out against the sleep they needed. When they woke up the next morning they were ready for the next fight. Life on the Front was too full of work and the risk for any one experience did not last for long.

Dawn was breaking when Nick came up to me saying,

"Lieutenant, I think there's something up with the tanks. They are coming from all parts of the front and getting together just back of our division. They will keep the Huns on the jump. If we have enough of them, we might roll into Berlin."

Gathering my men around I said," Attention men, before we get too excited about the tanks that will be leading us across the battlefield I will give you some information. A main proponent of tank warfare was Lt. Colonel George Patton Jr. He realized that the day of the horse cavalry was gone with the weapons such as machine guns, so he joined the tank corps. Our American Tanks were actually manufactured by the French Renault Company. The Germans were strong against the submarines, aircraft and artillery technology but slow to recognize the strength of the tanks."

Nick interrupted, "Sir, I saw tanks that were vulnerable to heavy weapons, fire, rough terrain, while breaking down sticking in the mud. Can we really depend on them for our safety?"

Another soldier spoke up, " I talked with a tank officer that described what it was like in a tank. It was hot, airless and bumpy. When reaching with their hands they would be burned by the hot engine."

I stopped him. "Now men get ready to follow the tanks, imperfect as they may be. They will crush bundles of brush, making bridges for our infantry to cross over. They clear the pathway for us to attack. Modifications will be made in the future. They are here to stay as weapons on the battlefield." The men stood up, saluted in unison saying, "Yes sir."

Under his breath Nick smiled as he murmured, "That's bully." For we Americans that means it is good.

As we gathered our weapons for the day's battle I silently prayed, "Holy Mary, Mother of God, please protect us. Amen.

The orders of the day were to commence by taking a French Battery to fire on the Germans. I took the men to blow up a portion of their trenches in just 12 minutes, to return to my men. Our next shoot was near Verdun where the ground had been fought over many times.

There were great holes 10 feet deep that were so close that they toppled over each other. This terrible shelling had taken place so many times that it was void of any vegetation while covered with broken guns and equipment of all kinds. Private Mason came up to me white as a sheet saying, "Sir, I just came upon more evidence of this war. Here are bones of horses and men in dried up piles. There are even boots with feet in them."

As I looked down I saw a soldier laying on his back, a gun bayonet pining it to the ground, with the gunstock sticking up straight.

"The Huns are coming," hollered Nick. As we headed into the battle I thought the Germans are leaving many dead men hanging on our wires, but they had plenty of them ready to take their places. The Kaiser is willing to fight to the last man, though he is not in the line of fire.

It crossed my mind of the excitement up and down our spines as we entered the war game. Now we felt it to some extent but we have seen enough that excitement may not be the correct word.

The Germans may be brave enough when they are shoulder to shoulder with each other but they have difficulty in thinking independently without an officer to help them. In the battle of Somme the Germans crews were chained to their cannons so that they could not run away. This is not necessary for the Americans.

Our men need brakes instead of spurs in the handling of our Doughboys. We can beat the Boche to a frazzle as we put our blood and guts on the line. Our men are better fighters than the Germans. I just pray that I am in the drive as the final gun is shot.

FOUR

❄

A new enemy is raising its ugly head in addition to what is going on in the trenches, the air and the sea. It is being called the Spanish Flu. It is affecting millions worldwide. Due to censorship, the papers reported the epidemic started in neutral Spain, which was not factual. It is said to have come from a U.S. Army training facility at Fort Riley, Kansas, to spread across the seas.

I am now reading a letter from Flora telling me that she and the children have now come down with the fever, chills and upper respiratory symptoms. They are now under quarantine. The American Red Cross is providing masks to millions to try to avoid the spreading of the germs. I am praying daily for their recovery. I feel so helpless being away from them.

The symptoms that Flora mentioned can go into pneumonia, which is killing mostly young adults. Now our troop in such close quarters and with weakened immune systems, are dying at an alarming rate without being injured by the bullets of the enemy.

Here is a little rhyme that I read in the newspaper:
I had a little bird, its name was Enza
I opened the window and in-flu-enza.

Trudging along the Chemin de Mort, which translates to "Road of Death," I saw how it got its name. It had been shelled a few hours before and I passed shell holes where men and horses were again exposed to the hot sun of 2 years under the earth, and the smell was terrible. There were no breezes to carry it away.

There was little time to ponder over our loved ones back home or even for grief over the injuries and deaths of our men. The American grit and steadfastness never wavered while the enemy was forced to retreat with heavy losses.

"Hot work," remarked Private Daniel as he swigged a mouthful of water from his canteen. He wiped off his dusty mouth saying, "I wish that I had that old bucket full of water from our well back in Texas. " In the trenches on the Front a soldier could not carry enough water to meet his daily needs. During an artillery bombardment you may not get water brought up from the camp for days. A full canteen was like gold in the middle of combat.

"Look out," yelled one of our men as the French threw up barrages over us, which looked like a consolidated 4th of July celebration in the U.S. This covered our position, which allowed us to move ahead.

"I can see that there'll be no monotony in our young lives today," observed Nick to Daniel. "With a fair share of luck we'll bring home the bacon," answered Daniel as he moved ahead.

Just hearing my men banter banter back and forth calmed my nerves. It is imperative that I show only the strength of an officer, always to be the leader of these brave men. These boys came off farms, factories, and offices across America to serve in our Armed Forces. Many of them are just 18 or 19 years old. After hurry up training, they are putting their lives on the line just hoping to win the war and go home to their loved ones.

Orders have arrived that we are to be ready to join in the major attack by the Americans. As we have held our positions for 3 days and nights the word was welcomed. Travel at night is necessary because the Boche planes and balloons can see us. This is not easy in the rain and mud. Our trucks and tractors cannot have lights.

One of our big trucks turned over rolling down a bank. Two of my men were badly hurt. As we pulled them out of the mud the driver said, "I am lucky to be alive. At least I am breathing again. Patch me up, give me another truck and let's go."

That is the kind of soldiers that we have brought over. Right now I am thinking of how some of my men got here when the call for our country to join the war effort across the pond. The draft board had a lot of work to do.

One of my men walked eighty miles to enlist, then the board turned him down due to his flat feet. They said that he wouldn't be able to stand a five mile hike. So he was drafted. Another man was almost rejected because he had a patch on one eye. He said, "Sir, I always shut that eye anyway when I shoot." He was accepted and is one of my top marksmen today.

The battle of Saint Mihiel is the first All American show in the war. It has now begun. Thank God we have strong air cover as we Yanks advance taking 15,000 German Prisoners. Sometimes I think that they are almost relieved to be taken into our camps in that they will have food to eat and a place to sleep. The prisoners have lost heart and are ready to end this war and go home. Their families are suffering as much as they are.

The fight is a birthday gift for General Pershing who turned 58 on this day. He sent out the statement, "The striking victory completely demonstrated the wisdom of building up a distinct army."

Just the word from our Commander gave us the courage to carry on. The Germans are losing heart. We are not. Sargeant Matthews yelled out, "Come on you sons of bitches! Do you want to live forever."

As the officer in charge of these men I know their frustration. They want to win this war too. It cannot end too soon. God help us in this battle.

Late one night Daniel came over to me holding a letter from his sister who was one of the brave nurses in this war. He read: "Brother, I hope that I do not come across you as we pick up wounded soldiers on the battlefield. As father may have told you I came over on a troop ship even before the American troops had arrived to assist the British Expeditionary Force.

"We nurses face many of the hardships that you all experience, yet must keep our heads up to be of service to you. It is heart breaking as we treat shrapnel wounds, infections, mustard gas burns, exposure and emotional trauma.

"Every day there are amputations, where all of the water would be heated on a small oil stove, which would also boil our medical instruments.

"I try to sleep a few hours at night hearing the sounds of the cannons nearby. At dawn I take a cold sponge bath and a splash of the cologne that our mother sent with me. It reminds me of the Saturday nights on the farm in the kitchen taking turns in the big washtub. Just little reminders keep up my spirits.

"The food is scarce for us as it is for you. Meat is not

usually available so we often eat beans, potatoes, corn bread and a little salt pork for flavoring.

"May God be with you my dear brother as I look forward to the time you and I will walk up to the farmhouse to be greeted by Poppa and Momma waiting with open arms on the front porch. Love, Your Sister."

Tears came down both of our eyes as he put the letter back in his pocket.

The shooting had stopped in the dark of night when Daniel piped up with "time to tip the bottle."

As we all got out the alcohol I had given this subject some thought and promised to write down why we needed to pass the alcohol here on the battlefield.

Our men have used alcohol and stimulants for centuries before going into battle. Morale had to be created.

Back in the States the Temperance movement was going on, but we needed our alcohol. We treated the movement with cynicism and hostility.

This night Daniel held the flask in his hand saying, "I wish those dry souls back home would lie shivering in the trenches, bodies shaking in pain and fear listening to the moaning of the wounded nearby and not crave a little relief from the ration of whiskey."

It is true that some of my men drank so much that they couldn't load their rifles or cannons. There is a fine line between drinking enough to settle the nerves and being too pissed off to be effective.

We craved sleep to prepare for battle. The alcohol acted as a sedative if only to knock us out for a few hours. We would lie there in the wet and cold while shooing off the rats that would crawl into our bedrolls. The flasks were passed, the snoring would begin and soon we would be ready as the sun was coming up to go back into battle.

25

FIVE

❧

Damn, what good are our guns when we have no ammunition. We have been waiting all day for the trucks to arrive. The roads are so broken up that one after another ammunition truck is stuck, unable to move.

This place is rotten. No one is buried. Horses and men lay dead along the road. Horses are the worst in that they are torn up with shellfire and open flesh. We buried 8 Huns that were killed in this ditch. Private Daniel slept with a dead Hun for a while this morning in a trench. He was too tired to notice him, but smelled him when he awoke.

Most of the day was spent burying our dead. About half of my men have Hun boots on them. They took them off the dead men, dried them off before putting on the ones nearest to their size. They are better than our shoes and leggings.

I had to scold some of my men today. They found a Hun that made a funny noise, then they stepped on his stomach. The poor good-natured chaps. I made each one of them find a Boche and bury him for punishment.

My kitchens arrived with plenty to eat so we are no longer hungry and are anxious to get into battle. The men are all now in their trenches for German planes are dropping bombs in the area. Luckily, they are not good at this for they are falling 500 yards to our right.

As we huddle in our trenches one of my men asked that we say the Lords Prayer together. We Catholics then added the Hail Mary and did the sign of the cross and we waited.

Many people call me Doc though I am not a doctor, but a regular soldier from Kentucky. However, I wish that I had the knowledge and medicine to cure flu that is taking many of our men. We are losing our officers and enlisted men daily. Lt. Phiffen and I are now in charge of the whole battalion in addition to my battery.

One third of my men who went to the hospitals never came back. I saw men who were too sick to march sit down on the side of the road and wait for an ambulance. When it did come some of them would be dead. Their bravery is pitiful to see but they are Americans at their best just hanging on so far from home and their families.

As we battled with our remaining men we finally had the Boche on the run. Two of my men were wounded seriously. My poor men though in the height of battle had nothing to eat for 36 hours and not even a wink of sleep.

We found some hard tack and a few cans of tomatoes in the woods. That night we mixed them together in a big can and enjoyed it to our hearts' content.

The darkness of the night set in with no sounds of gunfire for the moment. Lieutenant Phiffen brought out his whiskey flask and invited me to join him in some good old bar talk. I reached in my gear and wiped off the dust from my silver flask that was presented to me by my men a couple of months ago. The Lieutenant raised his flask and with a strong voice said, "Doc, you and I are not alone in leading our men. May God be with us for the remainder of this Great War." HEAR HEAR! and we took a long swig.

"Sir, the ammunition is coming today, but the time is uncertain. What shall we do?" asks Private Monroe. "I am not permitted to fire, as the ground chase is on." I answered.

I am not allowed to go on the roads with my big guns for the tractors are too slow. The Infantry have thrown away everything, blankets, packs, overcoats, all but their rifles and some hard tack. We are fighting the Hun while He tries to run.

Our trucks are passing loaded with men cheering and laughing. It is the greatest moment of my life. Wounded men are coming back as we give them the road and wave them on and on while they themselves are almost dead with wounds, thinking of nothing but victory.

This can't be war. It is the great rush of men who are crazy to pay the price for liberty with their bodies.

Holy Mary, Mother of God, be with the souls of our fallen soldiers.

May we have the courage of your Son as armor as we fight for the love of our country.

SIX

꩜

The quote from General William Sherman was, "War is hell, and whether a war is just or not, in the end the judgment will be up to God.

As a soldier, I have chosen to fight for our country, in this case joining our Allies across the pond.

There will be military heroes from this war that will have their names in the history books many years from now. The forgotten heroes that quietly are beside us in the foxholes, trenches and on the battlefields are the military chaplains. They did not carry weapons even at the Front. Most of the chaplains were Anglicans, but those regiments with predominantly Roman Catholic soldiers in them had Catholic priests too.

The Priest would read the burial services and frequently put themselves in great danger by administrating the last rites to men wounded in battle.

Some of my men, like me, were Catholic. We held services and received communion in churches that had been bombed. These churches were also turned into hospitals.

One of the most difficult orders that I would have to

follow was to destroy a beautiful Catholic church that was being used by the Germans in hiding. Tears flowed down my cheeks as I prayed for forgiveness.

Our battery had the privilege of having Father O'Malley join us for dinner and prayer before our next battle. After saying the blessing over our meal he spoke off the cuff saying, "Men, when I became a priest I was ready for anything God had in His plans for me. My fellow chaplains are right on the battlefield with you. We carry injured on stretchers, stepping over the dead, not knowing which step will be our last. War at its rawest is our domain, an ugly place of shattered bodies, severed limbs, broken heads and death. I only have the strength of a mortal, the rest is up to God. May God be with you men now and into eternity."

We took turns receiving the blessing from Father O'Malley, communion and with sprinkles of holy water we were ready for what lay ahead.

Over those months my men have bravely fought many battles. I note one now.

On September 25th I received orders to open fire on 4 German batteries situated in the Ravine de la Montagne near Beaumont for destruction. Our orders were to continue firing until further orders were given.

As we were firing, they tried to fire back but their attempts were feeble. Then a German Battery opened up on us using high explosives and guns. This was terrible while it lasted, four of our men were wounded. My brave men did not stop or hesitate but kept up their fire, quickly putting on their gas masks. The Germans shifted their fire while a French battery spotted them, silenced them so we were not bothered again.

The battle continued as we fired about 600 rounds on

the roads leading up the Muese north of Verdun. We took about 5,000 prisoners.

Damn, the Germans ruined my kitchen again. They hit it with two high explosive shells and some shrapnel This got our goat.

A French Colonel came and wanted me to give him names of 5 men for War Crosses for our scrape on September 25th that I have just described. I told him all of the men or none. All deserved the honor. They did not offer enough War Crosses for all, so we took none.

That is what the Brotherhood of our military is about. It is all for one and one for all. God Bless America.

SEVEN

❧

"What the Hell. Where am I? What happened?"

Nick told me this is what I said. It was all foggy to me. Next thing I recall is lying on the ground next to my motorcycle. This was my first ride on the Harley Davidson that arrived from America to be used on the Front.

Little did I know how fast it could go with just a twist of the throttle on the handlebar. The rock that I did not see brought me down in a crash that my men not far behind could hear.

Getting up with the help of my men brought me to my senses. My injuries were minor, which made me even more aware of the men that were actually hurt and killed in battle.

This experiment told me that I would be better off using trucks, trains and wagons to get to the front line when not marching.

"Hey Captain, you could have ridden on one of the British motorcycles called The Triumph nicknamed Trusty. But, they recommend wearing a strap leather belt and a Doughboy Helmet for safety," said one of my men. I was too doped up to know who it was.

Many men got off their horses to ride motorcycles to supply effective communication with the Front line troops. The motorcyclist also acted as military police.

My accident was caused by my stupidity. Maybe after the War I will get back on a motorcycle. For the few minutes before the crash it was great.

It was still dark as I was trying to get a little shuteye when I felt something wet and cold on my cheek. My eyes opened to see the face of a dog looking into my eyes. "What the hell" I yelled.

My men rushed over to me astonished at the sight of a large black and brown German Shepherd poking my face. Private Daniel was the first to speak. "Captain, This must be one of the War Dogs that are running messages across the Front.

The United States did not have organized dog units but borrowed a limited number of dogs from the French and British for casualty, message and guard duty. Daniel immediately called him Aundi after his farm dog Andy back home in Texas.

The messenger dogs like Aundi were considered real heroes of the War saving thousands of lives by delivering vital messages when phone lines were broken down or runners could be spotted and killed. Barbed wire, slit trenches, shell holes and chemical gasses were many of the obstacles these brave dogs faced. Many were wearing gas masks for protection from the poison gas in the air.

There have been stories told of dogs running thousands of meters delivering messages that saved units from destruction. The metal tube on his collar contained a note reading, "For God sake, Hold on! Will send troops to relieve you tomorrow."

All of us gathered around Aundi to tell him what a

good dog he was. We had to remove some barbed wire from his paws. He held up one at a time trusting us to take away the pain.

Aundi became our mascot reminding us of the comfort of our beloved pets back home. He helped to relieve the feverish strain of war and kept up the morale of the men in the trenches as it seems nothing else could do.

※

November 3, 1918. Ammunition came in today, but the line is uncertain and I am not permitted to fire, this ground chase is on. I am not allowed to go on the roads with my big guns for the tractors are too slow. The Infantry have thrown away everything, blankets, packs, overcoats, all but their rifles and a few hard-tack, and are fighting the Hun while he tries to run. Trucks pass loaded with men, cheering and laughing. It is the greatest time of my life; wounded coming back, give them the road and wave them on. They are almost dead with wounds, think of nothing but victory. This can't be war, it is the great rush of men who are crazy to pay the price for liberty with their bodies.

November 4, 1918.

Mothers, Saints, to give their begotten sons.
Sacrificed on God's altar.
In expiration.
Ah, the sins of the Huns.
As dawn's dew bathed rays, they go.
Courage of armor, love of right,
They win.

EPILOGUE

※

The last words written in the little grey journal were dated November 4, 1918. Why did they stop? My grandfather, Captain Joseph Twyman, was wounded. I do not know the extent of his injuries.

The war had just one week to go before the Armistice was signed and most of the United States military would be heading home, while my grandfather stayed on in France to assist with the reconstruction.

When he returned home in 1919, he was awarded the permanent rank of Captain. He was stationed at Fort Williams, Maine. After a few years he was assigned to Fort MacArthur, San Pedro, California, where he retired for the first time. As a civilian he worked for the Colorado River Aqueduct project, hiring men for labor. He was amazed at the strong football players who couldn't last for the day in the hot sun, where old skinny men were his most productive workers.

Another job that he loved was being a military advisor for Warner Brothers Motion Picture Company. He was able to take me to visit his old boss Pops Guthrie many years later at the studio.

When World War II came along, he was called back into service to be assigned stateside due to his age of 60. He would then hold the rank of full Colonel. I would travel with he and my grandmother across the country in troop trains from San Francisco to the East Coast. Even as a small child, I could feel the rumble of the train and hear the chatter of the men and women in uniform.

After the war he retired permanently to the good life telling stories to the grandchildren. It was my privilege to be raised by he and my grandmother from the age of one to adulthood. Every time we went through the gate of Fort MacArthur, the MP would salute him and I would proudly nod as if I had some importance. He and I had a lot of time to talk over the kitchen table where he told me war stories and of the military life. It is my gratitude that I wrote his book.

Anne Price

Made in the USA
Las Vegas, NV
25 January 2022

42293938R00028